D0201113

Kart Racing

Jay H. Smith

Reading consultant:

John Manning, Professor of Reading

University of Minnesota

Capstone Press

MINNEAPOLIS

C A P S T O N E   P R E S S

2440 Fernbrook Lane • Minneapolis, Minnesota 55447

Printed in the United States of America.

Library of Congress Cataloging-in-Publication Data
Smith, Jay H.
    Kart racing / by Jay H. Smith
    p. cm. --
    Includes bibliographical references (p. 45) and index.
    ISBN 1-56065-229-2
    1. Karting--Juvenile literature. I. Title.
GV1029.5.S64 1995
796.7'6--dc20

                    94-29510
                     CIP
                     AC

Table of Contents

Chapter 1

In the Action: You are There

Your dream of instant glory is gone. Face it–after the first two **heats** of your very first race, you're not exactly ready for the cover of *Karting Magazine*.

It's not all bad. In fact, you're doing well and having fun. You're exactly where you want to be–at the center of the action, racing your kart at the speedway.

The Green Flag

When the green flag signaled the start of the first heat, there were 17 karts in the race. Now, going into the third and final heat, only 11 remain. Somehow you have survived.

Your heart is beating fast. Your sweaty palms hold the wheel. You can hardly wait for the next green flag–and the final heat.

An Inch from Disaster

Before the race, you spent six months taking **open practice**. You drove at a slower pace, just to get used to your kart.

But open practice did not prepare you well enough. The first heat was almost a disaster. The speed was exciting, but you were not quite ready for it. When you reached the first corner, you spun out of control.

Fighting with all your strength, you just barely kept the kart from flipping over. While you were struggling, three karts passed you on the inside. You were now in last place, and ready to panic.

A Yellow Flag

Then you saw a yellow caution flag, meaning there was a hazard up ahead. One of

the leaders had dropped a wheel from his kart.
The wheel was now spinning across the track.

Everyone had to slow down. That gave you
a moment to take a deep breath and get
yourself under control. By the time the green
flag waved again, you were ready to make a
run at the pack.

Making Up Time

On the next **straightaway**, you had the kart going all-out at almost 70 miles (112 kilometers) per hour. You passed two slower karts. Backing off to 50 miles (80 kilometers) per hour, you made a clean, sharp turn. But you still drifted too wide, and one of the slow karts caught up to you again.

By the end of the fifth **lap**–halfway through the race–you were **broadsailing**. You were getting good at pitching the kart sideways and "sailing" through the turns. With better turns in each lap, you were just about ready to catch the other karts.

The White Flag

You were in sixth place when the officials waved the white flag. There was just one lap–a quarter-mile (402 meters)–to go. The first four karts were far ahead, and you couldn't possibly beat them. But you thought you could catch the fifth kart. You began to inch closer.

A Blue Flag

Since you were clearly moving faster than the fifth-place kart, an official waved a blue flag. This signaled the driver of that kart to make room and let you pass. He did, and you crossed the finish line fifth. Not bad, after that terrible start!

The Second Heat: A New Chance

All karters know about the importance of the start. With a strong start, a good kart driver can usually hold the lead.

Your improvement at the end of the first heat helped your confidence. You started well in the second heat. You shot into second place. Through the first nine laps, that's where you stayed.

The Checkered Flag

When the final lap began, you were only a foot (30 centimeters) behind. Then you made a move on the next-to-last straightaway. The surprised leader could not hold you back.

You broadsailed through the final turn like a pro. So did your opponent. He pulled even with you. Your two karts roared neck-and-neck down the final straightaway.

The karts were even, and now it was a battle of wills. At the end, your opponent turned out to be a little tougher. The checkered flag waved as he crossed the finish line just two inches (five centimeters) ahead of you.

Karting action is fast and furious as drivers maneuver for the inside track.

Angry with yourself, you vowed never to lose that way again. Your point total for the two heats put you in third place. You felt good about your chances in the final heat.

The Final Heat

In the **pit** before the final heat, you test your engine and clean your kart. You try to settle the butterflies in your stomach and prepare for this 20-lap heat.

You start off in third place as the heat begins. You keep that position for the first eight laps.

Then, just as you come out of a turn, you try to overtake the second-place kart. But you don't have the energy for it.

You thought you were in good shape, but the bumping and banging in those tight turns has worn you out. It's getting very tough to broadsail.

Little by little, you drop back. When the heat is finally over, you are in seventh place. Your point total for the three heats puts you in sixth place overall.

A Final Promise

At last it's over. You're dead-tired and your body aches, but you wouldn't have missed this for the world.

You silently make yourself a promise. Next time, your mind and body will be as tough as your kart. Next time you're going to win.

Chapter 2
Karting History

The first kart was built in California in 1956. Art Ingles, a designer of **Indy cars**, decided he would build a little car just for fun. He used some metal tubing to make a frame and added a 2.5-horsepower lawnmower motor worth $14.

He attached four wheels to the frame. Then he added a seat and a steering wheel. A bicycle chain connected the motor to the rear wheels.

At first, Ingles rode his little car around local parking lots. People were fascinated. They wanted to buy the cars. Ingles and his friend Lou Borelli built more karts, using their garages as workshops.

Another friend, Duffy Livingstone, copied the little car in his muffler shop. Soon Livingstone and his partners, Bill Rowles and Roy Desbrow, were also building and selling karts.

The Little Car Gets a Name: "Go-Kart"

In 1957, Lynn Wineland, a friend of Livingstone's, began calling the little car a "go-kart." The name stuck. Since then, the sport has been called go-karting or karting (although the "go" is hardly ever used anymore).

The First Kart Track

The karts were an instant success. They crowded the sidewalks and parking lots. Drivers and builders looked for a way to race their machines. In 1957, Desbrow, Rowles,

Livingstone, and Don Boberick opened the first kart track in Irwindale, California. It was called Go Kart Raceway.

Karters formed the Go Kart Club of America to set up rules for this popular new sport. Later the Go Kart Club would change its name to the International Kart Federation (IKF).

Karters take their places for the start of the next heat.

Chapter 3
Karting Today

Karts have changed since the days of Art Ingles and his friends. Specially made parts have replaced the pieces of wheelbarrows, chainsaws, and lawnmowers that Ingles used. Kart engines grow more and more powerful every year. Today they are made by professional engine builders.

Safety

Safety is important in karting. The IKF has strict racing rules, and no motor sport has a better safety record.

Digital speedometers tell the racer information such as average speed, top speed, and elapsed time.

Inspectors check the karts before every race. If a kart is not completely safe, it is not allowed to compete. There are even inspections at the end of the race, to make sure that the karts have not been damaged.

All karters must observe the safety rules and wear the proper equipment. If they do not, the result is instant **disqualification**.

All race drivers write their blood type and other vital medical data on their helmet and clothing. This information could save their lives in case of an accident.

The tracks have special barriers to protect spectators from karts that veer out of control. An ambulance or an emergency vehicle, with a doctor or **paramedic** on hand, stands by at every event.

Popularity

Karting continues to grow in popularity throughout the world. Although karting was born in North America, it now has even wider appeal in Europe. In fact, most world champion karters have been Europeans.

Chapter 4

Types of Karts

There are several different kinds of karts. The most popular types are sprint karts, speedway karts, and road-racing karts.

All karts have certain things in common. They lack a gearbox and a suspension system. And they all have a low center of gravity.

Sprint Karts

Sprint karts are very much like the original go-karts, but they are longer and more comfortable. The driver sits in an upright position. There are two engines, one on each side behind the seat. The fuel tank is under the steering wheel.

It takes skill and strength to hold the lead in a kart race.

Sprint karts race on smooth asphalt. Their tires, called **slicks**, have no treads. They are the best kind of tires for racing on this surface.

Some sprint karts can go as fast as 85 miles (135 kilometers) per hour on a straightaway.

Most reach speeds between 40 and 70 miles (65 and 112 kilometers) per hour.

Because sprint karts race on curving tracks at high speeds, they are an excellent way for Indy race drivers to train. Nelson Piquet, Emerson Fittipaldi, Al Unser Jr., Lake Speed, Alain Prost, and Darrell Waltrip are some of the great pros who started with sprint-kart racing when they were young.

It looks as if seven-time IKF champion Rich Hearn is about to join their ranks. David Terrier, the 1993 world karting champion, will probably also race Indy cars.

Speedway Karts

These karts are also known as dirt karts, because they run on dirt, not asphalt. Their tires have treads for better **traction** on the dirt.

Speedway karts carry special air filters to prevent dust from choking the engines. A fiberglass **fairing** in front shields the driver from stones or dirt kicked up by the other karts.

The top speed for dirt karts is 75 miles (120 kilometers) per hour. Most go 40 to 65 miles (65 to 94 kilometers) per hour.

Road-Racing Karts

Road-racing karts are also called **enduros**, because they are built for endurance. They carry more fuel than other racers.

Enduro drivers race at big stock-car tracks like Raceway Park in Daytona, Florida, or Watkins Glen in New York.

The driver lies down in a **horizontal** position. This reduces **wind resistance**, allowing the kart to go faster. Another interesting feature of road-racing karts is that the exhaust system may be adjusted while the karts are in motion.

The road-racing kart is the fastest type of kart to race. It can reach speeds of 130 miles (208 kilometers) per hour, although most go 85 to 125 miles (135 to 200 kilometers) per hour.

Chapter 5

Competition and Classes

Karts are divided into classes to assure fairness. There are over 70 classes altogether. They are set up according to the age of the driver, the combined weight of the kart and driver, the engine size, and the engine type.

Drivers must be at least eight years old to compete in sprint and speedway events. They must be at least 12 to participate in road-racing events. At 16, drivers start racing as adults.

Since 1974, professionals have competed in their own Expert Class. The Professional Kart Association has a special set of rules for this class.

Chapter 6
Equipment

You will, of course, need a kart. Before buying a new one, check with other racers and with karting schools to see if good used karts are available.

You will also need a helmet approved by the Snell Foundation, which tests and approves protective headgear. If your helmet does not have a shield, you will need to buy goggles. A neck collar, driving gloves, and ear plugs are also necessary. Most karters wear high-top sneakers, but leather boots are best.

The tension is high at the start of the race, when each driver must prepare a strategy to win.

Karters should wear clothing of thick leather or nylon. One-piece speedway suits have padding at the elbows and knees. Enduro racers should wear suits that are heat-resistant in case of fire.

Here are some tools and other equipment you will need: kart stand, starter with battery, tool box, gas can, drip pan, chain lube, tire pressure gauge, tire pump, fire extinguisher, and extra spark plugs.

Special trailers carry the karts from race to race.

Flags of Kart Racing

You will want to know the meanings of the flags before you try racing.

GREEN–race has begun; all clear.

WHITE–one lap left (used in sprint racing only).

WHITE with **RED CROSS**–emergency vehicle on the track.

BLUE–you are being overtaken by a faster kart. Make room.

YELLOW–caution–hazard on track. No passing. Slow down.

YELLOW and **RED** (waved together)–restart. Stop at start-finish line.

RED–stop at once. Track unsafe. Go to impound area.

BLACK–used by officials to signal particular drivers for mechanical problems, fuel or oil leaks, pit crew violations, or driving violations.

ROLLED BLACK–warns driver that his or her driving technique could result in disqualification.

CHECKERED–signals the end of the race.

Glossary

broadsailing–a speedway driving technique in which the driver pitches the kart sideways in order to make the turn

disqualification–to ban a driver from a race for breaking safety requirements or racing rules

enduros–road-racing karts that are built for endurance

fairing–the fiberglass shield in front of the speedway (or dirt) kart that protects the driver from gravel and mud

heat–a single course in a race. In sprint and speedway racing, three heats make up a race.

horizontal–parallel to the ground

Indy car–a high-powered, single-seat, open-cockpit car used in North American competitions such as the Indianapolis 500

lap–one entire length of a race course

open practice–practice sessions where non-racers can drive their karts

paramedic–a medical technician who can administer first aid in case of emergency

pit–area used for refueling and servicing of karts

slicks–tires with no treads

straightaway–the part of the track that is straight

traction–the friction that keeps a wheel from slipping or skidding

wind resistance–the force of moving air on an object

To Learn More

Barrett, Norman S. *Karting.* New York: Franklin Watts, 1988.

Cazin, Lorraine. *Karts.* Mankato, MN: Capstone Press, 1992.

Fichter, George S. *Karts and Karting.* New York: Franklin Watts, 1982.

Wilkinson, Sylvia. *Kart Racing.* Chicago: Childrens Press, 1985.

You can read articles about kart racing in these magazines: *Karting Magazine, Karter News,* and *Kart Sport.*

Some Useful Addresses

Canadian Go-Kart Track Owners Association
291 Clements Road West
Ajax, ON L1S 3W7

International Kart Federation (IKF)
4650 Arrow Highway, Suite B4
Montclair, CA 91763

World Karting Hall of Fame
4000 Speedway Boulevard
Talladega, AL 35160

Index

Photo Credits:

All photos provided by Larry Grace Photography.